# How 2 Hustle

Entrepreneurial Lessons, Principles &
Strategies taught from Street Hustlers in
America's Urban Underground

Raphael Wright
Urban Plug, L3C
ISBN: 978-0-9960943-3-7
LCN: 2016939143

ISBN: 978-0-9960943-3-7

LCN: 2016939143


Cover Design by Raphael Wright


www.how2hustlebook.com


Printed in the United States of America

This work is dedicated to my late cousin Shari, my late aunt Linda, and the city of Detroit.

# Foreword

This work serves as a concise entrepreneurial guidebook taught through the experiences of the street hustlers in America's hustle game. Intended for aspiring entrepreneurs from the hip hop generation, who are mostly black and Latino, poor and from the ghetto, How 2 Hustle is a treatise for those who seek entrepreneurial know-how. Interestingly, the game from this work is drawn not from Fortune 500 CEOs, other small business owners, or academic scholars, but from the streets which this target reader comes from. Without ignoring the many detriments these economic characters bring into our economies and societies, but putting capitalism in its most fair perspective, How 2 Hustle is a testament of pure, authentic entrepreneurship taught in a language of the street that any ghetto baby of this generation and beyond could understand, with relatable characters and situations which is much more penetrating than an approach outside of their environment.

This work takes wisdom from the many people that this target reader has interacted with on both a professional and personal level. Most importantly, they understand this talk. Hence, the learning process will be much easier. Please accept this work with open hands.

# America: Today in 2016

Between current times and decades prior, circumstances have been extreme for this target reader. The target reader, the products of the inner city and hip hop culture, have many social, political, legal, and economic barriers in front of them. Even in a world which has advanced so much, certain groups are still far behind. Economics is the key area of focus for this work, particularly in entrepreneurship. Enterprise has risen tremendously over the years for all groups in America, particularly those influenced by hip hop culture. However, success rates are dismal at best, leaving us extremely farther down in rank as it come to a small business presence. Our dismal economic foundation creates a bed of poverty, unemployment, little to no generational wealth, and ultimately no economic footing for the people of the group. Although the buying power of blacks and browns have surged to amazing highs, we aren't buying and selling with each other, which is also contributing to our down cause.

# Inspirations from the Past

With our current economic status in front of our eyes and the future not looking too bright, the burning passion to make a change and chance for my people arrive in my heart on a daily basis. I've never felt this type of motivation since I decided my fate so long ago. I grew up always wanting to become an entrepreneur, creating my own opportunities and the opportunities of others. Not having any mentorship or apprenticeship opportunities to help expose me to my future profession, I took an alternative route which was the streets. As an early teen, I came to the conclusion that enterprisers were independent and workers were dependent, that independence meant you could live life the way that you wanted to. I saw my parents working very hard for other people and that wasn't a life I wanted to lead for myself. However, the only examples of independence in the free market that I saw as a youth were the street hustlers. It helped that I knew them personally so I saw the good in them and their actions; when given nothing to make something of yourself, husting becomes the alternative which can provide that launch pad to make something of yourself. Does it solve all problems? Likely, no. But what it does is provide an alternative while mentally showing one he can achieve whatever he wishes to. If you can make a living in the underground markets, you can apply what you did there in the formal markets and make a killing. In perspective of this work, these improvisational, plan b masters display pure entrepreneurship that a person who was in my shoes could learn from. I didn't have to look outside my neighborhood for an internship because my mentors were right in my face. I jumped head first in the hustle economy and it made me who I am thanks to their mentorship.

The generation under me, who has it even easier and more difficult than me simultaneously, need all the assistance they can get in order to help bring stability, and prosperity to our people. In my way of helping, I am drawing from a very relatable well of knowledge, which was given to us from our fathers and mothers who changed the game in the late 70s and 80s in times far worse than ours. They hustled so that we could have it easier and their work deserves its rightful place in our history. Yet it will also guide us into a new wave of entrepreneurial success. Let our work in the future possess the same fire and passion as our parent's work in the past did. They hustled the hard way so that we could hustle the legal way. Let's make them proud.

# Letter 2 my Street Pops

Dear MC,

I love you bruh! You showed me the game directly and indirectly, not only in business, but in life. All that I am in the world has been influenced by your mentorship and for that I am very fortunate and appreciative. We are brothers by blood, but to me you will always be my street pops. Thanks for everything.

Love your Lil Bro,

Rafa

# Introduction

If you are reading this, you are about to learn how street hustlers make money in the hustle economy, and how their strategies and methods can teach you how to be an entrepreneur. The hustle economy and the formal economy are no different, neither are the characters involved. So, the hustlers who were the subject of my research are equally capable of teaching one how to become a successful entrepreneur.

# Before You Read

Those who are reading this should know that when I speak the word "hustler" I am speaking of both participants in the underground economy as well as the entrepreneurs of the formal world. Because this work is a comparison amongst the two, the word will be used to describe and name both entities.

# The Game

# Ch.1: The Game

The game is hard, dangerous, impenetrable, and only made for a certain type of individual. Only the strong survive in the entrepreneurial field.

**The Hustler/Entrepreneur** – Enterprisers. Individuals who take economic risks for financial gain and reward.

# Ch.2: Traits

True Enterprisers possess a combination of innate, teachable and divine traits.

### Innate Traits

The innate, unteachable traits are:

>**Realism** - Understanding and embracing reality.

**Independence** – A self-governing, self-reliant and self-starting attitude.

**Aspiration** - An intense hunger for more.

**Optimism** - The ability to visualize prospectively.

**Lion-Fox Complex (Aggressiveness & Cunningness)** - A combination of fearlessness, forcefulness, relentlessness, and dexterity that gives one the killer instinct to aggressively and swiftly advance forward and escape danger.

**Go-Getter Traits** - Stopping at nothing to accomplish goals.

**Risk-Taking Traits** - Embracing the possibility of loss with the hopes of gain.

**Shrewdness** - Sharpness and stern attitude towards handling business.

**Resiliency** - Ability to recover quickly from misfortunes and losses.

It is rare that one learns what is innate. Hence, the chances of being successful at enterprising without being born with these traits are not impossible, but less likely.

## Learnable Traits

The teachable traits are:

**Economics** - Understanding the concepts of supply, demand, scarcity and utility.

**Accounting** - Tracking incomes, expenses, cashflows, and profits.

Profits are ideally measured by volume (what quantity to sell, how many to sell to profit and how fast they must be sold for it to be worth it).

> **Sales & Marketing** - Effectively gaining exposure and closing deals.

> **Management** - Efficient coordination, monitoring and execution.

> **Gimmickry** - Techniques used to cut costs and maximize profits.

Everything that is teachable can be perfected, but only through strenuous activity and experience. These teachable qualities differ amongst the person, hustle, region, and circumstances.

## Luck

Aside of what is innate and teachable, which are both equally important, luck plays a pivotal role in the success of both hustlers and entrepreneurs.

# Ch.3: Risk

Risk drives enterprise. Those who are successful at enterprise understands and embraces risk.

# Ch.4: Money

## Time & Money

The focus should always be on making money.

## The Motivation

Money is the motivation.

# Ch.5: Work

The goal is to outperform the competition in all ways needed to stay in pocket.

## The Workload

Work every day, but not all day. When working, one should be improving the work and his network to provide the most to his clientele.

# Ch.6: Trust

Trust should be handled with extreme caution. Master the art of judgement which requires great analytical skills and fast thinking. Never settle too quickly and always be observant of who you are working with and what you are working for.

# Ch.7: Currencies

The three main types of currencies are:

Cash - Paper or coin currency.

Consignment - Credit.

> Barter - The trade of other products, services or favors.

Cash is the most coveted form of currency because it's a universal medium of exchange. Consignment should only be used with extreme caution. Bartering is good when trading for goods, services, and resources that's immediately needed or has a long term value.

# Ch.8: The Characters

**The Hustler** - The entrepreneur/enterpriser.

**The Customer** - Customers are purchasers of goods and services.

**The Plug** - Product supplier or connection to hookups and deals.

**The Middleman** - Middlemen broker deals between transacting parties for a fee, either between hustler/customer, hustler/hustler, or hustler/plug.

**The Hater** - Haters are those who pray for the hustler's downfall.

**The Competition** - Rivals in the same industry.

**Law Enforcement** – Interpreters and enforcers of the law.

# Ch.9: Types of Hustlers

Hustlers are either full time or part time. Of this kind, there are two types; the product hustler who sells products and the service hustler who sells services.

# Ch.10: Products

Clockwork products are priced cheap, sells fast and yields a modest profit. Slow-roll products are priced high, sells slow and yields high profits.

# Ch.11: Services

Petty services are priced cheap, have high sales volumes and yield a modest profit. Complex services are priced higher, have slow sales volumes but yield a high profit.

## The Summary

In essence, there are no differences between the formal and informal worlds when capitalism is the subject except legality. Hustlers and entrepreneurs are identical characters in society. Because someone hustles, it does not mean they are performing an illegal act, which also debunks the belief that everyone who operates within the law of economic regulation is upholding the best interest of humanity. Both the hustler and entrepreneur have bad qualities because they are chasing profit, which will bring out the best and worst in everyone. However, they are the drivers of our capitalist markets, which keeps us all employed.

# PART 2: HOW 2 HUSTLE

For one to enter into entrepreneurship, one must understand the game and what it takes to survive in it. Neglecting to grasp the understanding guarantees failure. Business is hell, no matter which eyes one is looking through. The end game is the same; money and success.

Once one has an understanding of the game, only then should be engage in any entrepreneurial activities. When starting, one has to crawl first, walking later, then running thereafter. The second section entitled *How 2 Hustle* explores the necessary philosophies, methods, and tactics of the most crafty, and successful hustlers/entrepreneurs in the game.

Highlights of this section is the innate intensity in the characters in this first stage. Similar to when you make your first dollar, the excitement and passion at this stage should be channeled into appropriate, forward aggression which will carve out a place for any hustler.

# Starting Up

# Ch12: Entering the Game

## The Objective

The objectives of a hustler entering the game is:

Soak up as much game as possible.

Master surviving.

Secure a reliable plug or employer.

Get in where he can fit in.

## Barriers of Entry

Barriers of entry into the game differ depending on the trap, timing, and the hustler's position. Some traps are more different to enter than others, timing has to be perfect, and the hustler have to be solvent enough mentally, physically, and financially to have a fair chance at being successful.

## The Workload

When trying to get on, the workload is intense and never-ending.

## The Mental

There is nothing to lose at this point, but everything to gain which fuels the intense hunger needed at this phase in the game. Small timers are highly optimistic, seeing everything for the taking and acting without a sense of consequence. This optimism, mixed with inexperience, can cause either over-aggression or fear. In essence, this hustler is the least tamed and most vulnerable in the hustle game.

## Where to Start?

Roads already paved are ideal for new hustlers because of the proven clientele base. However, a new customer to one means an old customer to another, so the hustler must be ready to fight to get on. An alternative would be to take new work to a new area that's untested where the hustler will have to perform analysis and research. Either way, small timers just starting out have to get it from the mud.

## How to Start?

Small timers can either take the roads already paved or pave a new path. Either way, it's smart to place yourself next to the competition and show how your work is better. Also, either way, small timers just starting out have to get it from the mud.

## Risk

Risk is perhaps the highest during this stage, so this hustler must be prepared to handle the pressure.

## Start Up Costs

Operation costs in the beginning are perhaps the highest, between selling, marketing, and sweat equity. When small time, everything usually costs more because they lack connections and clout.

## Fox-Lion Complex

**A prince must imitate the fox and the lion, for the lion cannot protect himself from traps, and the fox cannot defend himself from wolves. One must therefore be a fox to recognize traps, and a lion to frighten wolves**

**- Niccolo Machiavelli (The Prince)**

Small timers must be more lion-like than foxlike; more aggressive than crafty, particularly when trying to win over new customers.

# Learning the Game

Small timers must learn about:

> **Industry -** the particulars of a given field or trade.

> **Environment -** the objects, conditions and occurrences in which the hustler is surrounded.

> **Customers -** the purchaser of goods and services.

> **Competition -** Rivals.

> **The Law -** the rules and orders of an area.

Understanding industry, environment, customers, competition and the laws gives small timers the competitive, comparable, and tactical advantage in the hustle game.

## Supply & Demand

Understanding supply and demand is vital to successful enterprise. Some hustlers are masters of creating demand and driving supply, while other hustlers are masters of exploiting supply of work that's in high demand.

## Layers

No one person is indestructible, so both the hustler and the entrepreneur need layers to block them from competitive attacks, law enforcement raids, and shifts in customer taste. No layer is indestructible either, but the more layered the enterpriser is, the more prepared he'll be for rainy days.

## Contracts/Agreements

In the game, one should invest in his own protection. Hence, hustlers must always make sure he has a clear understanding of all values and considerations when making a deal with anyone and to take serious measures in ensuring all agreements considered are met from himself and the opposite party.

## Cash & Carry

The small timer must use his own money to get on. When self-funding their own ventures, they are making mistakes and taking losses on their own dime, building a foundation from their own cash, and can move, work and grow at their own pace.

## Communication

Effective communication is crucial for hustlers. Being able to properly communicate costs, prices, benefits, etc. is vital to business success.

## Building Credibility & Trust

The hustler builds credibility through his reputation. Hustlers with bad reputations can never build trust with many. A great reputation is built through great work and great service at all times.

# Ch.13: Learning

The learning process either begin on one's own or through an apprenticeship. Self-taught hustlers have been known to be the more venturing, resilient breed. The graduated apprentice hustler has been known to be more skilled in the trades.

Regardless of the advantage, both hustlers will make mistakes, but the learning process must not be ignored.

# Operating

The upcoming section entitled **_Operating_** explores principles and strategies of day-to-day operations of a hustler's business. Mostly everything in this section entails how to manage, network, market, and sale. Other parts detail safety and physiological aspects of customers, and competition.

By this time, the hustler should have an understanding of the come up stage through direct experience and is only improving, adapting, and growing by this part of this work.

# Ch.14: The Transaction Process

The transaction process in the hustle game is as follows:

> The hustler makes work (products and services) available.

> The hustler markets work to potential customers.

> Customers purchase work from the hustler, generating revenue for the hustler.

> The hustler sells out and has to re-up. Then, the process starts over again.

## Interference

Within the transaction process, there will be the possibility of interferences which affect how the hustler makes money. Hence, the hustler's job is to strive to eliminate as many obstacles as possible.

## Receiving Payment

The hustler must always seek full payment for his work. If the customer makes a partial payment, the hustler must sell partial work. The hustler must accept [1]shorts with extreme caution, warning the customer to come correct on the next transaction. If the customer fails to do so, never do business with them again.

## Regarding Credit

The hustler must accept credit with extreme caution, making sure they are offering credit to someone who is very creditworthy. If the customer does not pay his debt, the hustler must first try to

---

[1] Shorts - Urban slang term for accepting a partial payment for a product or service.

every diplomatic way to get repayment. If the hustler cannot get payment at this point, not do business with this customer again.

## Consequences for Credit Default

Consequences must be enforced to those who violate this concept. The amount of the default determines the severity of the consequence. For small amounts, simply ending the business relationship would be sufficient. For large amounts, action must be taken to avoid a total loss. Hustlers should always use diplomacy in dealing with delinquent customers to keep hopes present that they will catch up to their debt. If diplomacy fails, customers must be dealt with to serve as an example for others who may think about attempting to default.

## Bartering

The hustler must always get the better deal in a barter transaction. If the customer is offering $100 barter for $100 work, the hustler should not accept. If the customer is offering $150 barter for $100 work, the hustler should accept.

# Ch.15: The Product Hustler

For product hustlers, what is of main importance is: access to a reliable plug (connect) and prices. If a product hustler has a solid plug, with great prices, the product hustler can offer a great deal. Aside from this, the types of products sold are of importance, for if the hustler is peddling an unfavorable product, neither the plug nor the price matters.

# The Re-Up

The [2]re-up must be spent on inventory only, and should be [3]sold-up at all times to keep it working.

# Investing

In the beginning, the hustler must invest the re-up and all of the proceeds to boss up. As profits increase, the hustler does not have to invest all of his proceeds.

---

[2] Re-Up - Urban slang term for the funds used to by businesses to purchase inventory.
[3] Sold-Up - Urban slang term defining when investment funds are invested into inventory or an investment that will produce a profit.

# The Constant Flip
*Turn one into two.*
*Two into four.*
*Four into more.*
*-Old Street Wise Tale*

The hustler should be focusing on flipping his money as many times as possible in the beginning, allowing his investment to grow, accumulate compound interest so that he can boss up.

## Consignment

Small timers must stay away from consignment and only work on his own money because he does not have enough business to take on credit.

**A strong word called consignment. Strictly for live men, not for freshmen. If you ain't got the clientele say hell no cause they gone want they money rain, sleet, hail, snow.**

**- Notorious BIG (Ten Crack Commandment)**

## Buying & Selling

Work is bought low and sold high. [4]Work is usually bought from a plug, or private seller in special cases.

## Picking the Hustle

Hustlers must choose a product that is highly demanded, easy to sell, easy to understand, and easy to explain.

## Smart Hustles vs. Dumb Hustles

Hustling is risky. Smart hustles are risky, but rewarding. Dumb hustles are risky with no reward.

## Securing a Plug

Finding a plug is simple, requiring only research. Securing a plug requires trust. Nothing builds trust

---

[4] Work - Urban slang term for inventory.

better than money. So, after asking around and finding a plug, approach the plug with cash to do business and business will surely be done.

## Gaining Trust from a Plug

The hustler must simply be himself and always bring money to the table to gain trust with the plug.

## Dealing with a Plug

The hustler and the plug must be fully honest with each other, with the hustler paying the agreed price and the plug giving the agreed portion.

## The Ideal Plug

The ideal plug is honest with what he offers and consistent with his delivery.

## How many Plugs should a Hustler have?

This hustler should strive to gain a relationship with as many plugs as possible to ensure the success of his business. When one plug is unavailable, another plug will be available.

## Ch.16: The Service Hustler

This section elaborates on the concepts, processes, and strategies for service hustlers. For service hustlers, what is of main importance is: mastery of a given trade, and prices (how much should the hustler charge for his services). Service hustlers must focus on truly mastering his craft, for the more he knows, the more he can corner the market.

## Choosing & Mastering the Trade

The service hustler must choose a trade in which he is already skilled. The service hustler masters his trade only through experience, and activity.

## Cutting Corners

The hustler must never cheat his business because he is only cheating himself.

## Concentration

The small timer should focus on a single hustle, and as he can handle other hustles he can then venture out.

## Competition

Depending on the circumstance, the hustler can either cooperate with competition or eliminate competition. If it would be more beneficial to the hustler if he comes to an understanding with the competition, then he should cooperate. If it would be more beneficial to the hustler if he gets rid of the competition, then he should eliminate.

## Cooperating with Competition

Cooperation occurs when two hustlers come to an agreement to avoid conflict.

## Eliminating Competition

Eliminating competition is when one hustler ends the business of another hustler which is sometimes a necessity to continue his business. In many cases, either it is you or the competition.

## Haters

During this stage, being hated on is highly unlikely. However, there is always someone being hated on, so the hustler should strive to observe the hating process to prepare him on how to maneuver through it.

## Spotting the Hater

Haters are most likely those who are closest. Therefore, hating cannot be observed through words but through actions since mostly everyone will say only the right things.

## The Law

The best method of defeating the law is avoidance, doing whatever is necessary to stay out of their sights. If caught, this hustler must take whatever punishment he is given and either try again or give it up.

One should know that what is lawful is not always what is morally right. Therefore, this work is not an encouragement to stay in accordance to all laws but to stay out of the sights of the law, which is not always the same. Those who are successful in enterprise are not usually those who are following all laws, but those who are good at staying out of sight of the law.

## Accounting

The hustler must track incomes and expenses in simplicity.

## Paper Trails

Paper trails are written record that if landed in the wrong hands could damage the hustler's business so they must be used with extreme caution. When used, records must be accurate and safety secured, away from the wrong hands.

# Losses
## Can't be a Boss if ya never took a loss

### - Rocko da Don (Losses)

Losses are unavoidable, so the hustler must embrace this reality and use losses as lessons for improvement. However, if losses are a continuous occurrence for the hustler, he should reconsider his business.

**Gained fame not by winning, but by losing.**

### - Don King

# Appearance

The hustler must look trustworthy to get on and stay on. If one looks shady, he will never get on. Appearances should fit the trade.

## The Hustler's Selling Philosophy

For the small timer, the more he gives, the more he receives.

**The best givers are the best receivers.**

**- Russell Simmons**

# Ch.17: Customers

Understanding customers and their habits is of central importance to the hustler. The hustler should focus on conducting business with the right customers, which are customers who he can build trust with, and will be a consistently returning customer.

Customers, by nature, are only loyal to those who offers them the most value, so the hustler must offer that value to gain and keep customers.

# The Customer's Buying Philosophy

All customers want a deal. New customers want a deal better than their current deal. Existing customers wants to be kept happy.

## The Customer's Mental

What matters most to customers are **(1) price, (2) quantity, (3) availability, and (4) quality.**

## Price

Usually, cheaper priced work is the most enticing. The higher the quantity purchased, the cheaper the price.

## Quantity

Price considered, the higher the quantity offered, the more enticing the deal is to the customer.

## Availability

Considering price and quantity, products and services priced competitive are only enticing when readily available. Availability is measured based on whenever the customer wants them.

## Quality

**Great work sells itself**

**- Street Wise Tale**

All other factors considered, high qualities are highly recommended. However, lower qualities are just as sellable as higher qualities, depending on the circumstance, like droughts.

## A Deal

A deal is an enticing price, quantity and/or quality. Price and quantity is more enticing than quality but quality increases the value of the deal.

## Approaching New Customers

The hustler must be aggressive and direct when approaching potential new customers. The truth is that only a fraction of new sales leads will buy from the hustler, and only a fraction of those will be converted into regular clientele.

## The Customer/ Hustler Dynamic

Most likely, a customer usually has options with who they shop with. The customer rank these options as follows:

**Primary Supplier** – This hustler is the customer's first option to shop with, which is a gift and a curse. A gift because they possess the highest level of trust with a customer, which can yield consistent income and profits. However, this hustler can lose the customer if he disappoints just one time. So, the hustler must always fully satisfy his customers or he will lose them.

**The Backup –** This is the customer's second option, in the event that the primary option is unavailable. This option will always be necessary as an alternative for when the primary option does not satisfy. If the primary option is constantly unsatisfying, the backup could replace him. If this hustler becomes the primary option, he must consistently satisfy or he will lose clientele.

The small time hustler is better suited as a customer's backup where he can get in where he fits in, leaving the opportunity to steal customers from established hustlers.

# The Hustler's Upsell

The hustler must always upsell the advantages of his work. If price is the most important factor, then the hustler must upsell his prices. If quantity is the most important factor of business, then the hustler must upsell his quantities. If availability is the most important factor of business, then the hustler must upsell his availability. If quality is the most important factor of business, then the hustler must upsell his qualities.

## Samples

The product hustler that is selling clockwork goods should offer samples to potential customers to entice interest. The service hustler that is selling petty services should offer sample jobs or a portfolio of their work to entice interest. Hustlers of complex trades, products, and services can only truly rely on reputation to entice interest.

## The First Customers

The ideal first customers are those that the hustler has access to already, like family and friends. Note that family and friends are not great long term customers because of their sense of entitlement, which will eventually affect business. However, they are great at word of mouth advertising.

## Types of Customers

The types of customers in the hustle game are:

**The Ideal Customer** - One who completely trusts the hustler and will only conduct business with him, is easy to do business with, shops around the hustler's schedule, is willing to travel, pays upfront with cash, never uses credit, and spread the word about the hustler. The hustler has to keep these customers happy by all means.

**The Regular Customer** - One who displays average customer characteristics. The regular customer trusts the hustler enough to do business with, but is not loyal enough to only spend with the hustler. This customer could conduct business like the ideal customer would but this customer lacks the loyalty and dedication to do so, therefore, the hustler should supply this customer only when called upon by the customer.

**The Worst Customer** - This customer does not benefit the hustler in any form and must be avoided at all times.

## Dealing with Customers

The relationship between the hustler and the customer must be business only, never personal. The hustler must be respectful, yet shrewd. If the hustler is too nice, he will be taken advantage of. If the hustler is too shrewd, he will chase customers away. If this relationship is built on personal emotions, the relationship will never last. It is the job of the hustler to establish this understanding because customers will always strive to make things personal to get their way.

## Getting Cheated by Customers

Often times, a hustler will engage with a customer whose intentions are to cheat. Although these types of customers are unavoidable, the hustler can guard himself from these customer's intentions.

# Ways Customers Cheat

Ways that customers can cheat a hustler are:

**Currency Cheating** - Intentionally not paying the hustler the agreed amount, or paying with counterfeit funds.

**Product Cheating** - Intentionally trying to receive more product than the customer paid for, or stealing.

**Service Cheating** - Intentionally trying to receive more services than the customer paid for.

## Avoiding being cheated by Customers

The best defense against getting cheated by a customer is being upfront about buying and selling agreements, double checking currencies, and standing firm on agreements. Hence, a hustler should only sell what is paid for, and make sure he is receiving the agreed upon tender.

# Ch.18: Prices

The most important aspect to hustling is price. In theory, the hustle economy is a segment which provides the best prices for products and services because the absence of supervision and regulation, which brings higher costs. The hustler who can gain access to demanded products and services at a great price, it is estimated that he will fare better in the hustle game.

## Prices

Because of the cheaper costs of doing business in the hustle game, prices are cheaper in the hustle game for both the hustler and the customer.

## Street Value Prices

Street value prices are retail prices for the hustle game. High street level retail prices are the equivalent to convenience store retail prices to customers. Low street level retail prices are the equivalent to warehouse store retail prices to customers or small time hustlers.

## Wholesale Prices

Wholesale prices are low per unit prices based on bulk order, sold by a plug. The plug may require the hustler to buy 100 pieces for $50 per unit for an item that retails for $100 per unit. Wholesale prices are very low so the hustler has the ability to make great profits.

# Ch.19: Contentment

The true hustler has a hunger for more that will never allow him to be comfortable with where he is. If the hustler ever becomes content with where he is, he should not be hustling.

## When to Boss Up?

The hustler can boss up when he truly understands the ins & outs of the game and his trade. The hustler should strive to boss up when his reputation grows and clientele starts to increase. Throughout all stages of the game, it is easy for one to be misguided by early success or failures. Because all tables can turn at lightning speeds, hustlers must remain logical and humble throughout his career to have a better vision as to when he should boss up.

# Managing Funds

Perhaps one of the most important skills to master as a hustler or entrepreneur is the ability to effectively spend and save money. Spending is evitable in life. However, it is how you spend your money determines success or failure. If one is conscious about what they are spending their funds on and have a spending plan, they will be better positioned for operation and long term success.

The ability to save is pivotal in enterprise. Having a surplus funds opens the door to multiple options; either to expand or enhanced security in droughts. Mastering the saving process is key to any economic dealings.

# Ch. 20: Managing Spending

Mastering spending requires control and discipline. In regards to spending, a hustler must strive to spend smart, efficiently, and to a minimum, making budgeting vital to a hustler's business. Successful spending habits should start in the come up stage, when money is usually dismal, so when incomes and profits rise, the hustler will be able to successfully manage.

## Common Costs

Common immediate personal costs for hustlers are:

- Food
- Utilities - Lights, water, and gas
- Transportation - Gas money
- Communications - Phone and internet

## Maximizing Spending

Maximizing spending is when a hustler spends money only on necessities. Aside from necessities, a smart hustler will always shop for the bargain.

# Ch. 21: Becoming a Stackmaster

Stacking is the saving process. If nothing else, stacking is the one skill that every hustler has to master in order to maintain.

## The Best Places to Hide Savings?

The hustler must store his money in the safest places possible. For many, banks are the safest. For others, holding their liquid funds at home is the safest. It all depends on the hustler.

## What affects Stacking?

Factors that affect the hustler's ability to save are: low profits, high expenses, reckless spending, and unexpected expenses. Hence, the hustler must strive to control all of the above factors (profits, costs and discipline) in order to maximize stacking.

## Low Profits

When incomes or profits are low, the ability to save are low. Hence, the hustler should always strive to make more income or profit, for the more money that the hustler brings in, the more he has to work with.

## High Expenses

When living expenses are high, the ability to save are low. Hence, the hustler should always strive to lower expenses and maintain those low levels into the future, for the less money that the hustler spends, the more he has to work with.

## Reckless Spending

When the hustler has reckless spending habits, the ability to save are lowered. Hence, the hustler should always strive to control spending for reasons that are not of necessity, for the less that the hustler spends, the more he has to work with.

## Unexpected Expenses

One function that savings serve is to pay for unexpected costs, like medical or home costs that are outside daily or monthly expenses. Hence, the hustler should always strive to save as much as possible to be prepared for these occurrences. However, when these events occur, they drain savings.

# Stacking by Stage

Every hustler's goal should be to save as much as possible. However, each stage warrants different stacking capabilities, which are.

- **Come Up Stage** - The hustler on the come up can only save small amounts, if that. Hence, the start-up hustler should strive to save at least 10% of his earnings each month, if not more.

- **Survival Stage** - The established hustler has more capabilities to save versus the startup hustler. Hence, this hustler should save more than the startup hustler. It is recommended that the established hustler stack from 10% - 25% of his earnings each month, of not more.

- **Boss Stage** - This hustler has the best prospects to save. Hence, this hustler should maximize his savings, striving to save at 25% of his earnings monthly, if not more.

## Other Important Stacking Tips

Lastly, the hustler must remember:

- **When to pay himself** - Since incomes and profits are small for the startup hustler, he should pay himself last, after all costs and expenses are covered. When incomes and profits are moderate to large, costs and expenses are stabled and better controlled, the hustler should pay himself first, assuming that all costs will be covered.

- **How to Stack?** - The hustler should save in easy intervals, such as $5, $10, $20, $25, $50, or $100. The hustler should avoid saving in difficult intervals, such as $2, $3, $4, etc.

· The only reason for the hustler to touch his stack is for emergencies only.

# Business Lessons from this Stage

The formal parallel between the startup hustler and startup entrepreneur pulls the following similarities:

**Hunger & Ambition** - Both the hustler and the entrepreneur in their infant stages exhibit an intense hunger and ambition to get on and get ahead.

**Aggressiveness** - Along with hunger and ambition, both the startup and the startup entrepreneur has to exhibit exceptional amounts of aggressiveness when trying to establish themselves in their respective games.

**Building** - Both the startup hustler and the startup entrepreneur should be working to build clientele, relationships, and connections to grow their businesses.

**Learning** - Both the startup hustler and the startup entrepreneur should be striving to learn as much as possible while small time, so that when they boss up, their knowledge, along with experience, will better equip them for the coming adventures in business.

# Surviving

Not many make it to this stage, whether you are street hustler or a formal entrepreneur. Surpassing small time status is hard work. Statistics show that most new small businesses fail and also remains true for most street hustlers; most hustlers remain small time. Of all that is required to come up in the hustle and formal economies, those traits, skills, and attitudes have to be elevated in order to make it to this stage, which is the stage for established hustlers with clientele and connections.

The central action set and attitude for success amongst this hustler and entrepreneur are that of craftiness and cunning, using one's brain (mental), and less aggression (physical). Contrary to the start-up hustler and entrepreneur, who has nothing to lose, these characters have something to lose. Hence, this hustler must make smarter moves to not only get ahead, but to keep what he already has. Some may say that this hustler's tactics for gaining, protecting, and preserving are underhanded, but when the central goal for this hustler is ensure his operation's survival, no rock should go unturned.

# Staying On

# Ch. 23: The Established Hustler

## The Objective

The objective of the established hustler should be to:

Protect what he has gained.

Increase clientele

Create a durable advantage

Maximize profits.

Network to stay competitive, boss up or position for an exit into legitimacy.

## Barriers of Survival

Surviving is perhaps more difficult than starting up because there is more to lose at this stage.

## The Position

This hustler has built a foundation with clientele, knowledge, experience and a network. This hustler is making more money than before, but still has more room to grow. Hence, this hustler still has everything to gain, but now has something to lose.

## Fox-Lion Complex

This hustler must exert more foxlike qualities, while staying hungry in order to survive.

## The Mental

This hustler understands boundaries and the consequences of crossing them, so he operates in a more controlled matter.

# Guarding One's Gains

**Don't shoot em, kill em.**

**- 50 Cent**

Ensuring the safety of one's current gains is a new element to the hustler. Previously, when the hustler was on the come up, protecting something was of minimal importance because of the minimal value to protect. However, this hustler has made gains and must incorporate plans and strategies to keep them safe, such as savings, clientele, connections, and most of all, his life.

The hustler must protect his gains by any means necessary. If attacked, the attacker must be eliminated completely.

## Growing

The hustler should grow from his own incomes. Other factors of growth are more customers and cheaper expenses.

## Competition

More money equals more competition. Cooperation, elimination and the criteria for accepting both remain the same.

## The Haters

If hated on, the hustler should continue to work but with caution. The hustler must never attack hate, but only defend himself from attacks by hate.

## Concealment

The hustler must never speak of his business to
anyone.

**Never let no one know how much dough you hold
cause you know the cheddar bring jealousy
'specially if that man fucked up, get your ass stuck
up.**

**- Notorious BIG (Ten Crack Commandments)**

# Ch. 24: The Product Hustler (Pt. 2)

## Consignment

The established hustler has the ability to take

consignment if he has clientele that spends money

fast and consistently. The hustler must also have

the ability to cover the balances of consignment in

case of losses. Plugs can charge a higher cost for

credit than for paid goods, but the hustler will

profit 100% because he is not putting up any money during this process.

## Cutting Work

**I'd buy two pounds [of marijuana], which is thirty two ounces, and I remember pouring it on my table and dividing it into thirty three ounces.**

**- Bill Maher**

Cutting work stretches profit by shortening or diluting products and services without the customer's knowledge. Without cutting products, the hustler can buy work at 100 grams for $100 and sell 1 gram portions for $2, grossing $200 and generating $100 profit. When cutting products, the hustler can buy work at 100 grams for $100 and sell 0.8 gram portions for $2, grossing $250 and generating $150 profit. Cutting generally are applied to clockwork items where weight or pieces are important to the selling of the product. Whole items cannot be cut.

Without cutting services, the hustler can perform a service for $100. When cutting services, the hustler can perform a service for $100 and create another job through sabotage that would generate more income.

The key to cutting work successfully is doing it without alarming the customer. Cutting too much will show and the customer will shop elsewhere. The cut should never affect the appearance of the work or the customer will be alarmed.

# Ch. 25: Operating (Pt. 2)

This section outlines the operating practices of a successful established hustler. Different from the hustler that's on the come up since this hustler is focusing on not only making gains, but also maximizing current opportunities, while preserving what he has already gained. Introduced in this section is the concept of gimmickry, which to some is a form of underhanded trickery to maximize profits. However, the practices of an established hustler is parallel to that of mostly all successful formal business and enterprise worldwide. In fact, the gimmickry of a hustler is no rival to that of formal capitalism.

# The Hustler's Selling Philosophy

This hustler maximizes opportunity by cutting costs and stretching profits. Hence, the less the hustler gives and the more he saves, the more he receives.

# Types of Costs

The two types of costs that hustlers incur are personal and business. Usually, personal costs are the highest of all costs. The highest business costs for the product hustler would be inventory. The highest costs for the service hustler would be equipment.

# Middlemen

The hustler should buy from middlemen only when their plugs are unavailable because middlemen will usually charge more for work. If this hustler comes across a great deal, he can sell it through a middlemen. Service hustlers should never sell through middlemen. To make an extra income, this hustler can take on work as a middleman if circumstances allow.

In regards to products, the established hustler has a better prospect to middleman products because of his reputation and connections. The hustler who knows many, and has a solid reputation has the ability to virtually anything to anyone. In this case, however, the products does not belong to the hustler.

In regards to services, the established hustler has a better prospect to middleman (subcontract) services because of his reputation and connections. The established hustler doesn't even have to be skilled in a selected trade to sell the service to a customer. Hence, selling another's services and charging a "finder's fee" would be easy. In fact, when being a middleman between services, it is advised that the hustler announces to the customer the finder's fee to destroy any confusions or difficulties in the transaction, such as: questions that the hustler cannot answer and explaining why the hustler is not performing the service, yet is handling the transaction in the first place.

## Improving Relations with the Plug

The more money the plug makes from the hustler, the more important the hustler becomes to the plug.

## Gimmickry

Gimmicks are sales schemes that entice attention, while allowing the cut to occur. Without gimmickry, the hustler can buy work at 100 grams for $100 and sell 3 gram portions for $10, grossing $330 and generating $230 profit. When using gimmickry, he can buy work at 100 grams for $100 and offer the deal of three 0.8 gram portions for $10, grossing $410 and generating $310 profit.

> **The Hand is quicker than the eye.**
>
> **- Sleight of Hand Magicians**

## Keeping Customers

If new customers have to won over, existing customers has to be well maintained. This hustler has to do what is needed to keep his customers happy or he will lose them.

## Pricing & Deals

If the customer stays in an area where work is plentiful, the hustler must offer a deal to entice interest. If the customer stays in an area where work is less supplied, the hustler must sell his work at high street level retail. If the customer stays in an area where work is scarce, the customer should be charged higher than high street value retail. The more customers buy, the cheaper their price should be.

At this stage, the more the customer buys the less he receives. However, the customer must not know that. This shortening can be hid through cutting and gimmicks.

## Regarding Dissatisfied Customers

Regardless of the issue, if the hustler's ideal customers are dissatisfied, he must do whatever is needed to fix the problem. Depending of the issue, if the hustler's regular customers are dissatisfied, he should fix the problem. Regardless of the issue, if an unfavorable customer gets dissatisfied, the hustler should not fix the problem, using the issue to break ties with the customer.

Common issues that will cause dissatisfaction are quantity, quality, and delivery. The best way to eliminate this confusion is to always provide what's demanded in these aspects of the game.

## The Seasons

The hustle game has seasons that expands or swallows money making opportunities. The hustler must plan differently according to the season. Regardless of the season, demand never decreases, so the hustler must still work through all seasons, just differently according to the season.

## Floods

Floods are seasons where either work and/or money are in high supply. The hustler should use floods to gain more clientele. During floods, the most important factors of business that the hustler should consider is price and quality.

## Work Floods

Work floods are times where work is in high supply, so the hustler should strive to offer the lowest price around. Low quality or fair quality work can be sold, but it would only benefit the hustler to offer the highest quality work possible.

## Money Floods

Money floods are times where customers have excess cash. The high supply of funds causes customers to spend more, so the hustler should be focused on maximizing profits. Hence, the hustler should raise prices and provide the highest quality of work possible.

# Droughts

Droughts are seasons where either work or money are in low supply. Most hustlers have difficulties earning during droughts, but all hustlers have the opportunity to maintain. The craftier hustler can create lucrative opportunities during droughts. During all droughts, the most important factors of business are price and quality.

**Slow motion is better than no motion.**

**- Old Urban Wise Quote**

# Quantity

Quantities should be adjusted to the customer's spending power. During floods, the customer's spending power is higher than usual, so the hustler should offer higher quantities than during droughts when spending powers are reduced.

## Money Droughts

Money droughts are times where the customer's money supply is low, so the hustler reduce quantity. If the hustler sells work at 1 gram for $5 during favorable times, he should sell work smaller than 1 gram for $5 during droughts.

Qualities could be fair, given the price, but it should only benefit the hustler to offer the highest quality possible.

## Work Droughts

Work droughts are times where work is scarce. During work droughts, the hustler should focus on staying afloat first. During work droughts, high qualities are rare to find, so practically anything will sell and at a higher price, with higher quality work being even higher priced.

## Product Work Droughts

Product droughts are when products are scarce, so the hustler must focus on securing a plug with the highest quality work around. Any quality will sell at a higher price, but the highest qualities will sell at a higher premium, yielding higher profits.

## Service Work Droughts

Service droughts occur when services are scarce. During service droughts, the most-hungry hustlers will take on an increased job load and charge a premium.

# The Summary

This hustler has built a foundation that he has to protect by all means, while still pursuing more. Aside from protecting his operation(s), this hustler is still working to expand and grow, which would yield higher profits. This expansion and growth requires elevated level of dexterous, foxlike qualities. The hustlers who exert an exceptional level of fox and lion qualities will boss up.

## Business Lessons from the this Hustler

Like hustlers on the come up and novice entrepreneurs, experienced participants in the hustle economy share the same objectives as a seasoned entrepreneur: growth and survival. Having built a foundation that is solid, both the established hustler and entrepreneur are trying to maximize their ventures, while at the same time protecting their current gains.

Different from small timers who must exert high levels of aggression to get on, experienced workers use their wit and craftiness (their brain) to stay on and get ahead even further. Both have to master the manipulation of circumstances from their resources and reputation.

Specific between the objectives of the established hustler and the established entrepreneur are:

Maximizing profits through sales

Minimizing business costs through connections, which gets them needed items for cheap (product, equipment, etc.)

Minimizing personal costs through extreme budgeting, conscious spending, and modest living

# Bossing Up

The third and last section of street hustling is the boss stage. These characters possess extremely high levels of everything that a hustler should have. Contrary to what one would think, a hustler in this position, which is a position of a leader, a manager that's responsible for putting others on, and amassing huge profits, has the capabilities of entering the formal economy as an entrepreneur. This hustler has the money, the experience, and the connections to be successful in the formal economy.

There are many bosses in the hustle game, those who have surpassed both getting on and surviving and is enjoying sizable profits. Most likely, these characters are not active in the daily operations anymore but are more focused on delegating and making the hard decisions. For one to have access to a boss, much is still be learned from him.

# Ch. 26: Bossing Up

The established hustler with a highly exceptional level of ingeniousness has the ability to ascend much higher on the hustle game and can run operations that bring in massive profits. For product hustlers, getting to this level require a bulletproof reputation, highly resourceful network, a massive clientele and access to cheap priced, highest quality work. For service hustlers, getting to this level require a bulletproof reputation and a massive clientele. This hustler earns big, but has the largest probability to lose big. Hence, this hustler's objective is to strive to keep doing things that make money and avoid what causes losses, as well as to protect what he has.

## Putting Others On

Aside from being established and highly lucrative, perhaps the greatest skill that a boss has is creating opportunities for others.

## Hiring Workers

Hands-on work (sales, marketing, planning, etc.) is usually not pleasurable or required of a hustler at this level. Hence, bosses hire employees to handle those tasks.

## The Ideal Worker

The ideal worker must be ambitious and willing to work. The worker's main objective is to perform whatever is required from the boss. Workers respect the game and their position in it. They don't strive to outshine the boss, but instead indebts himself to the boss to receive the mentorship and blessings that bosses offer.

## The Ideal Boss

The ideal boss must be fair, honest, and giving to their workers. The boss's main objective is to protect his gains and the platform he has created for his crew. The ideal boss pays what is owed on all occasions and work to elevate others.

## The Leadership Styles of the Boss

There are two types of leaders in the hustle economy:

> **One who leads from the front** - This leader is always in the front of the movement and operation. This leader is comfortable when his ego is constantly stroked, making it a requirement that his

crew publically praise him, which in turn makes him work effectively.

**One who leads from the cut[5]** - This leader is best behind the scenes, working in the shadows. Completely the opposite of the leader who leads in the front, this leader wants to be appreciated for what he gives to his crew, but would prefer that there are no public praises of his contributions.

It would be optimal to have the best traits of both the front-leading boss and the rear-leading boss. Charisma is perhaps the best trait of a front-leading boss. Shrewdness is perhaps the best trait of a rear-leading boss.

---

[5] Cut - Behind the scenes.

## The Working Style of the Boss

The boss's work consists of delegating. Bosses are less hands-on in sales, marketing, and manufacturing because people are hired for that.

## Avoiding being the Outlier Boss

To avoid resentment amongst the team, the boss should push the identity of the team, meaning if the boss is fly, the team must be fly as well. If the boss is dirty, the team must be dirty as well. Avoid being the boss who create different mentalities amongst his team. Avoid following a boss who will leave his team dirty in times where he is clean.

# The Exiting Strategy

At this stage, this hustler should have accumulated the funds and network to start as many enterprises as he wishes. Hence, the objective should be to exploit the resources that have been acquired and plant your feet into the ground of entrepreneurship.

Legitimizing does not end the hustle. The same skills, principles and strategies used in the underground markets will position you for success in the formal markets.

# Ending Thoughts

The growth and evolution of the hustle game (informal economy) is adjacent to the growth and evolution of the formal economies worldwide. Because our formal economies are flawed and manipulated to only benefit few and take advantage of the majority, the hustle game, a fair and wide-open economic alternative will always be available for whoever desires to self-start and secure their survival.

Regardless if you are operating formally or informally, the stats are the same. Some will make more. Few will get rich. Nonetheless, all have to work for their keep.

For the inspiring entrepreneurs who come from similar beginning as I have, the road will be increasingly difficult. However, this hip hop generation have advantages that our fathers of the 80s and before that did not have. We must use our advances and our innate gifts which were passed to us from our hustling fathers and create the economic foundation that will provide the needed opportunities for our people so that we can truly live stable and prosperous. We were born with the hustle. Now, it is time to unleash it for the world. To all of the young hustlers in the world today, please thank your fathers who blessed you with the gift of hustle, for they provided me with what I needed to complete this work. I hope that this piece will help guide, inspire, and motivate only the upmost positive and forward action for you. I hope that our generation use the energies of hustle for the greater good and put as many people on as possible. It is not getting any easier, so we have to make things happen for ourselves, and our people!

Wala Kubisha Mbio

Do Not Knock the Hustle

# Hustling Sources

Losby, Jan, Marcia E. Kingslow and John F. Else. "The Informal Economy: Experiences of African Americans." The Aspen Institute Sept. 2003. Print.

Edgcomb, Elaine, and Maria Medrano Armington. "The Informal Economy: Latino Enterprises at the Margins." The Aspen Institute Sept. 2003. Print.

Neuwirth, Robert. Stealth of Nations: The Global Rise of the Informal Economy. New York: Anchor, 2012. Print.

Snow on tha Bluff. Dir. Damon Russell, Michael K. Williams. Perf. Curtis Snow. Screen Media Films, 2012. Film.

Notorious BIG. "Ten Crack Commandments." Life After Death. Bad Boy, 1997. Compact Disc.

Demetrius "Big Meech" Flenory. "Time and Money." Time and Money, 2002. Web.

Blade Icewood. Stackmaster. Dirty Glove Entertainment, 2004. CD.

Venkatesh, Sudhir. Off the Books: The Underground Economy of the Urban Poor. New York: Penguin, 1987. Print.

How To Make Money Selling Drugs. Dir. Matthew Cooke. Perf. Susan Sarandon, Russell Simmons, Curtis "50 Cent" Jackson, "Freeway" Rick Ross, Eminem . Tribeca, 2013. Film.

De Soto Polar, Hernando. The Other Path: The Invisible Revolution in the Third World. New York: Basic, 2002. Print.

Machiavelli, Niccolo. The Prince. New York: Penguin, 2008. Print.

The Alpo Story. Dir. Troy Reed. Perf. Alberto Martinez, Azie Faison. Warner Bros, 2005. DVD.

Rocko. Losses. A1 Recordings, 2010. CD.

"Don King Quotes." Think Exist. Think Exist, n.d. Web. 24 Feb. 2009.

Simmons, Russell. Super Rich: A Guide to Having it All. New York: Gotham, 2011. Print.

"Sleight of Hand." Wikipedia. Wikimedia Foundation, n.d. Web. 23 Feb. 2009.

The Players Club. Dir. Ice Cube. Perf. Ice Cube, LisaRaye McCoy and Jamie Foxx. New Line Cinema, 1998. Film.

Unknown Author. Slow motion is better than no motion

"Big Meech Interview." Youtube. Google, n.d. Web. 24 Feb. 2009.

Greene, Robert. The 48 Laws of Power. New York: Penguin, 2000. Print.

Jones, Milton, Raymond Canty and Julius Justice. YBI: The Autobiography of Butch Jones. Detroit: H Publications, 1996. Print.

"Episode 288." Real Time with Bill Maher. Season 11. Writ. Bill Maher. Home Box Office, 2013. Web.

# The Author
## Raphael Wright

Raphael Wright is a social entrepreneur, investor, and author from Detroit. Currently, Wright is the CEO of Plug'd Media, a hip hop media collective which focuses on music, film, literature, art, apparel, and interactive media. Plug'd Media is the publisher of How 2 Hustle and the creator of HustleMania Shirts, a streetwear brand. In 2016, Wright, along with a group of other entrepreneurs and business professionals, started Urban Plug L3C, a social enterprise dedicated to economic empowerment in urban Detroit through entrepreneurship, personal finance, and investing. The organization is starting BOSS Academy, a teenage entrepreneurial bootcamp.